My Shortness is my Tallness

Jose K. C

31 Success Formulae

For:

❖ Excellent school/college assembly speeches
❖ Outstanding essays
❖ Effective value education lessons
❖ Inspired living
❖ Good life skill practices

Rich in:

• Anecdotes from great lives
• References to world classics
• Folklore wisdom
• Variety of quotes

MY SHORTNESS
is
MY TALLNESS

Jose K. C.

authorHOUSE®

AuthorHouse™
1663 Liberty Drive
Bloomington, IN 47403
www.authorhouse.com
Phone: 1-800-839-8640

Proof-read by: i. Mr. Tashi Gyeltshen
ii. Mr. Choeda

First published by AuthorHouse   10/05/2011

ISBN: 978-1-4567-9629-7 (sc)
ISBN: 978-1-4567-9630-3 (ebk)

Preface

Today's citizen is a netizen, thanks to the internet revolution. Caught in that cyber-net, man has lost the age-old interpersonal intimacy. A personal handshake or a hug is distanced by the mobile phone and the long-honoured calligraphy replaced by e-mails and chats. The latter are good achievements though in their own right.

Amidst and despite these achievements, we stand stunned at the loss of the grandeur and warmth of the heroes of the yore: Jesus, the Buddha, Florence Nightingale, Martin Luther King, Pemi Tshewang Tashi, Gelong Sumdar Tashi, Mahatma Gandhi, and Abraham Lincoln, to name a few. Those raw citizens—not yet netizens—had what we sorely lack. Our great grandparents were early risers, for example; they were duty-conscious, punctual, stoic, and spontaneously charitable. Today, we are late risers. Most of us are lethargic, materialistic, irritable, and unscrupulously selfish. To top it all, there is an alarming role-model deficit in our midst. We often thus feel that something is missing despite the affluence and plenitude—our moral landscape is eroded, resembling the Eliotean wasteland.

Against this backdrop, these thirty-one success formulae are launched as a small beacon of the much-needed guidance for the budding youngsters through stories and role models' experiences of the past years.

The idea for the title of the book is from a verse by a popular Malayalam poet, Kunjunni *maash,* and I have an essay on it.

Having grown personally and professionally in Bhutan the past twenty-five years, I submit this booklet as a humble silver jubilee souvenir.

Jose K. C.

Contents

1

Word Is Not Word

A six-inch-long tongue may kill a six-foot-tall person. King Henry II got frustrated with his one-time close friend, Archbishop Thomas Beckett of Canterbury, when the latter refused to dance to the royal tune. In his rage, the king thought out loud, 'What sluggards . . . Who will rid me of this meddlesome priest?' Hearing this, four knights, ever ready to put the king's wishes into action, went and killed Thomas Beckett. That was on 29 December 1170. King Henry repented the consequence of his casual, unintentional thought in sack-clothes and ashes.

No wonder that Buddhism stresses right speech. A six-inch-long tongue may also lift a baby, an adolescent, or an adult to great heights. For example, little Thomas Alva Edison's mother read out his teacher's letter: 'Your son is intelligent and studious.' In fact, the letter actually read, 'Your son is addled and unteachable.' But the great mother was unlike the average parents, who would not only read the letter as it was with relish but would add fuel to the fire by scolding the child such that his self-esteem meter would dip fatally.

That little Edison soon became a great inventor the world would not forget. Later, he acknowledged: 'My mother was the making of me. She was so true, so sure of me, and I felt I had some one to live for, some one I must not disappoint.' That was the metamorphosis of the so-called addled student into a creative genius. It was the sheer power of words.

It is pertinent here to think that we are given only one tongue and two eyes and ears each because we are to see more and hear more than we speak. That's why the Bible warns us, 'You must account for every word that you utter' (Matt. 12:36). Only the human species is endowed with the power to speak, so that skill of speaking should be used befitting human nature. Some appear superhuman, some just human, and some subhuman in their use of words.

Once an enemy slapped Lord Buddha—an unprovoked assault. Ananda, his close disciple, could not stand it. But the Buddha explained, 'In fact, the man came to talk his anger out. But as he came near, he could not. So he slapped me. Come on. We should understand his predicament.'

The next day, the assailant—now very remorseful and repentant—came to apologize and to become the Buddha's disciple. The enlightened one said, 'You didn't slap me. Between yesterday and now, I have been reborn several times. You had, in fact, hurt another person.'

Behold the disarming forgiveness of a superman, couched in compassionate words. Such words often seep into our marrow, and even a sinner is reborn as a saint.

Good talk fills us and our listeners with positive energy. Our outlook becomes positive, and our lives are filled with brightness. Then life on the whole becomes worth living.

2

Monkhood to Monstrosity

Unlearning monstrosity is difficult. Thus reverting to monkhood, which one once gave up, is hard. Habits die hard because they are addictive.

A fable has it that a solitary monk in his hut in the jungle grew fascinated by the handsome, glittering sword which a fleeing soldier had left there. Despite his best resistance, the monk was drawn to the sword with its well-wrought hilt.

One day, he simply swung the sword in the air, and it shone and outdid lightning. Gradually on his strolls, he held it and casually struck the shoots on the way. Down fell the innocent, tender leaves, neatly cut. What neat levelling! The monk was thrilled to the backbone. He then tested it on a timid hare that came that way. The cut was so easy and perfect. He laughed, seeing the quivering, severed hare's head. Soon he gave up monkhood, emboldened by the strange, hitherto unknown omnipotence granted by the sword.

The impact of the company of even an inanimate sword on austere monkhood is an irresistible lesson parents and educators must take home. Our children are like wet cement: that which falls on it leaves a lasting mark. Let good things, good friends, and good habits fall on children.

Everyone, especially children, pick up bad habits such as substance abuse when their contacts so orient them. But counselling them back to being social well-fits is toil indeed.

The rotten apple metaphor in Shakespeare's *The Taming of the Shrew* is famous: 'There's small choice in rotten apples.' Here the speaker, Hortensio, says that the shrew, Catherine, will be a bad influence on the hero, Petruchio. The influence of friends, media, Internet, and cinema on children is unquestionable. That is why Bertrand Russell is against Rousseauism, which grants absolute freedom to children during their upbringing.

The immortal Russian writer, Dostoevsky's Raskolnikov in his *Crime and Punishment* is a law-student with good intentions in life. Napoleon is his role model, and he believes that the dictates of conscience can be overlooked when the ends are good. A philanthropist at heart, he commits a double murder. Soon, he writhes under a gnawing guilt complex. At last, Sonia Marmaledova, herself a sinner, appears as his redeemer. She makes the healing touch on Raskolnikov's sore soul. See the positive energy of a therapeutic touch by a friend in need. A new habit of admitting one's sins developed in him.

The folk tale of the crooked dog's tail is often quoted by village elders to underline the force of habit. Unhappy about the crookedness of his pet's tail, the master decided to make it straight by inserting the tail in a straight tube. The poor dog carried its imprisoned (for unrighteousness) tail for two months. After that period, the expectant master untied the tube. Much to his chagrin, the tail went back crooked.

The force of habit is so strong that unlearning it is really hard. Prevention is better than cure. Be a vigilant guard against bad habits and company.

3

A Stone in the Sore

A piece of bread buttered on one side. How does it land on the floor if it slips from your hand? The butter touching the dirty floor? The unbuttered side touching the floor? Perhaps fifty-fifty?

The pessimist mum scolded the eight-year-old Peter, 'You good-for-nothing brat. I expected that the bread would drop off your clumsy hands. The butter would have all the dirt of the floor. Like father, like son.' The absent father too got a pretty share of the blame.

Hearing the noise, her younger sister rushed there and enquired, 'What happened, Peter, my dear? Tell me.'

Poor, bewildered Peter looked in the direction of the ill-fated bread slice. His aunt bent down and saw that the buttered side was on the top. Oh, it was not that bad! But Peter's mummy was not ready to give up. 'Where, where? I'm sure the buttered side will be down, taking in all the dirt.'

When her sister showed it otherwise, the pessimist reasoned, 'Now I know—you must have put it that way. As usual, you will support your nephew.'

This is the picture of a negative person. The jaundiced eyes see things yellow. Negative attitude is like the stone in a sore, preventing its healing despite best treatments.

A biker once rides off the road. Out of the many sores he had after the accident, one still remains painful today. Medication has healed all other injuries except this teeming sore. He got good treatment from the district hospital, indigenous hospital, and a week-long religious ritual. However, the effect remained tantalizing—painful at times. He was puzzled now.

One day a friend of his volunteered to dress up his wound. While cleaning the mischievous sore, he found a small stone lodged in. He removed it, cleaned the area, and then applied some medicines. The healing was fairly fast and permanent.

Keeping this little hardness of negative attitude in life, our quest for peace of mind by various means, including religion, is bound to fail. Be positive and then go for joy and peace. You will find it.

How can a cynical mother-in-law get joy if she is prejudiced against her daughter-in-law? 'Is this how your mother taught you to sweep the floor?' The mother-in-law was sure that she would corner her foe by showing some dust in the corner. The daughter-in-law replied, 'Mom, today your daughter, not me, has swept the floor.'

Seeing her charge boomerang, the mother retorted, 'Then you must have made a second sweep after her. That's why there is still some dust left over.'

A similar kind of cynicism, prejudice, and negative attitude echo in the words of a girl in class XI named Betty, responding to a question why she was practising tae kwon do: 'I must be equipped enough to defend myself from my would-be husband.'

The rest is history. Betty had a wrecked marriage. You are what you think. Negative attitude is like a closed room. Inside, you will feel stuffy and soon irritated.

John Hay's poem 'The Enchanted Shirt' sums up the joy of a positive beggar, who

> *whistled, and sang, and laughed and rolled*
> *On the grass in the soft June air.*

4

A Day, a Twenty-Four-Hour Suitcase

Albert, Robert, and Bill took part in a packing contest. They were to pack suitcases of the same model with the same clothes provided.

After the start bell, Albert relaxed for a while and then started packing, still in a relaxed state. Towards the middle, he hurried and packed most clothes unfolded and crumpled. At the end bell, he struggled and shut the suitcase, a few clothes hanging out helplessly.

Robert also relaxed at the start bell, saying 'There's enough time.' Before long he started packing. He folded the clothes neatly, packed them to a tee. At the end bell, he panicked and shut the suitcase, at least 20 per cent of the clothes still left untouched.

Bill was different. At the start bell, he swung into action and started packing. He was slow and steady sometimes, fast and steady at other times—but steady through and through. Like Robert, Bill packed the clothes in order, but he completed the work. Better still, he had a couple of minutes for an overview of his work before he shut the suitcase at the end bell.

I may be an Albert, you may be a Robert, and your friend may be a Bill when it comes to time management. We all have the same suitcase, namely the twenty-four-hour day. If we are given the same work in quantity, quality, and nature, we end up as different performers at the end bell.

Some of our Alberts and Roberts scream out, 'No time!' Such frustrated screams are heard particularly at deadlines—for instance while submitting our homework, projects, and reports. How is it that Bill completes the work and still has time for an inspection?

Albert and Robert's problem is that they don't grab time. Learn this phrase: *carpe diem*, meaning 'seize the day'. Time, like the tide, cannot wait for us. Successful businessmen are sure that 'time is money' more than the naïve equation 'money is money'.

An angry Albert may burst out, 'How can all be the same?' A cool Bill may reply, 'All cannot be the same. But I'd invite you to grow into a better time manager and then passing the examinations, making good speeches, and performing well in the interviews become easy.'

5

Three-Minute Titanic Delay

Life is short, but many of us make it shorter. How? Life becomes shorter when we waste our time.

Life became short to those 1,600-odd passengers aboard the *Titanic* on 14 April 1912. The officer on duty in the engine room attended the non-stop phone bell three minutes late because he had been busy. 'Reverse immediately; a huge iceberg just in front,' was the message from the control room. By then, it was too late—the fatal three-minute delay!

Sages say that a stitch in time saves nine. Stitch your tear at the very beginning—in time. If so, you need not have to stitch nine times later. If the cricket in the fable had not sung away its time, it would not have needed to beg of the industrious ant for some food.

Be an early riser. Do your homework on time. Eat and sleep at the right times. Fight tendencies of procrastination. Be it the very common chores in life such as washing the plates, bathing, readying the next day's clothes—develop a habit of timely execution. You will turn them into good habits. Habits, whether good or bad, die hard. Once good habits are formed, they follow you to the tomb.

Be punctual. Punctuality builds an image for you—an impressive social standing. An unpunctual person is a thief of his own and others' time. Of course, unpunctuality is most often not deliberate, Arnold Bennett says. Often we waste our time by living in the past or the future. Oliver Goldsmith advises us to live in the present; let the past be buried and the future be born slowly.

We should spend some of our morning thinking about good things in nature and life, besides the blessings of God. This will refresh and energize us for the day. If we get up worried and tense, the day is bound to fail. We become what we think.

The long and the short of it all is that we should be very frugal in our use of time, or else we will have to pay dearly for the weakness called temporal mismanagement.

Ask a bad manager of time, 'Will you be able to cope better if the day were thirty-four hours—ten hours extra?' She may say yes, but the truth will turn out to be no. A poor manager's activities expand with the available time—popularly known as Parkinson's law. Be a good manager of time and prove that Parkinson's law fails in your case.

6

Question Marks Signal That . . .

Teacher: What do you cut grass with, during your SUPW (socially useful and productive work) in the school?

Student: With a sickle, sir.

Teacher: You know, there is committed SUPW and there is unwilling SUPW.

Student: (*Giggling*) Mostly unwilling SUPW.

Teacher: Hats off to your honesty. Well, what do these sickles in such an unwilling SUPW look like?

Student: Like sickles, sir.

Teacher: Good; you are using the law of identity in math, like AB = BA. But have you noticed that the sickles look like question marks?

Student: Sir. Very true, sir. But . . . but sickles always look like question marks, don't they?

Teacher: Well! You're not wrong. But the point is, in an unwilling SUPW, you half-cut or quarter-cut and then relax . . . and then suddenly half-cut . . . In the process, the 'question marks' in the sickles are visible. On the other hand, in a committed and interested SUPW, the sickles 'shine in use', as Tennyson says. So you cannot see the question marks in the sickles.

Student: (*With a glow of understanding.*) Yes, sir. What does it mean, sir?

Teacher: The meaning and message we will come to later. Now, what do you, the unwilling learner in your study—mostly nodding and prostrating to the open book—look like?

Student: Like a clumsy student, sir.

Teacher: Excellent; good use of the right adjective, 'clumsy'. Now, suppose you are a professional photographer, about to snap the clumsy student's photograph from a distance. To you, what does this student look like from a distance? You know it . . . come on . . .

Student: Yes, sir, I know. Like a question mark.

Teacher: (*Shaking hands with the student.*) How clever! Be ready for another situation. The fatherless baby in the mother's pouch on her back. You, the photographer . . . tell me. What does this baby look like?

Student: Much like a question mark.

Teacher: Wonderful! You got the point.

Student: But sir, don't all babies in the pouch look like that?

Teacher: That' right. But an illegitimate birth often doesn't get the care, warmth, and affection that's due it. Besides, the dispirited, rejected mother adds to its question mark look.

Student: Sir, very nice similes. But what is the message, sir?

Teacher: Love what you do and do what you love. Unwilling people are question marks to themselves and to the society.

7

Dogs Teach

Did Shakespeare write the following line for dogs? 'Love sought is good; but given unsought is better.'

The canine's unsolicited, unconditional love for its master tempts me along that line. But then, dogs loved their masters even before Shakespeare. Even the velvety touch of the toy dog's nose soothes aching souls; my friend Karma Dorji feels in one of his poems.

Conditions are set, agreements are signed, and documentary evidence is created in business. Love by its very nature cannot be business, so love is unconditional, like the dog's. If love is unconditional, a marriage certificate can be a satire on love. But the satire becomes necessary when man does not qualify as dogs in terms of love and devotion.

The Canadian Christie Blatchford, in one of her disarming narrations, *Dogs and Books*, says dogs and books are the only friends in life who are ever available and never demanding. Test your dogs for their love—throw them, kick them, relegate them, reject them, starve them, tether them for long periods. After the test, they caper about you, climb on you, lick you, and whine in love. They are there at your beck and call. They pass the test with flying colours—no grudges harboured, no wrongs remembered. Unconditional love is overwhelming and inundating.

No wonder the Romantic, Lord Byron's heart bled at the death of his pet dog, Boatswain, in 1808. The master had been so attached to his Boatswain that he had nursed the rabid dog to its tomb. 'Epitaph to a Dog' is a famous piece.

> Near this spot/ Are deposited the Remains
> Of one/ Who possessed beauty
> Without vanity, / Strength without Insolence
> Courage without Ferocity,
> And all the virtues of man/ Without his Vices . . .

Perhaps human vices entailed conditions, and conditions are chains. They presuppose doubts and fears. They obstruct the spontaneity of the love flow. When has man, in his phylogeny from a quadruped mammal to a biped mammal, felt the need for conditional love? One sees a retrograde evolution in man that runs parallel but backward to the phylogenic evolution to Homo sapiens.

Does a dog, of any time and clime say that

I shall love only if you are beautiful
I shall love only if you are rich
I shall love only if you make me a pretty home
I shall love only if you love me back . . . and so on?

No, except perhaps some human dogs!

8

Be a Miser in Your Judgement

The fable has it that a lion, in mortal fear of the crowing of a cock, sought the help of an elephant. The elephant could not but laugh. 'How's it . . . how's it that the king of the forest is afraid of the nut of a cock? Woha . . . Woha . . .' He trumpeted a laugh but not for long.

The elephant suddenly stopped. A tiny mosquito was orbiting around him with its nasty whine. He said, 'If this little thing gets into my trunk, I'll be doomed.'

'You mean this silly mosquito?' the lion said, reciprocating a laugh and a half.

A hare, not very far away, heard all this and laughed his lungs out. In fact, he wanted to control himself for fear of the two giants close at hand. But laughter is like that at times, hard to brake . . . He laughed so much that his upper lip tore. Thenceforth, the hair has been tri-lipped.

That is why the ancient wisdom tells us, Don't judge, and then you will not be judged. Don't try to take the speck out of your friend's eyes before you clear your eyes of the log lodged there, Jesus advises us. Can the mother crab demand of her young ones forward movement when she herself moves sideways?

Many of us are like the mother crab. We want our children not to smoke, when we ourselves smoke. We are unpunctual, but we want our students to be punctual. We are late risers ourselves, yet we preach the sermon of early rising. Such hypocrisies often boomerang.

Learn from the lion. He knew about his weakness and so sought his friend's help, though he later succumbed to the temptation of sarcasm. The latter, instead of sympathizing and helping the lion, was sarcastic, and so he and later the hare got their due.

Great sages like the Buddha, Jesus, and Krishna were epitomes of compassion and understanding. Empathy and understanding save. All saviours of the world are personifications of compassion.

Don't point fingers except when it helps. Nobody is perfect; we are the stuff that dreams are made on, Shakespeare tells us in *The Tempest*. We are a mixture of strengths and weaknesses. Acceptance of our weaknesses, and respect for others as they are, are the first steps towards positive growth.

9

To Forgive Is Godly

The hyperactive Cutie disobeyed his dad the seventh time that day. The dad's chord of patience snapped, and he beat Cutie and sent him to bed unkissed.

Soon, Dad felt bad and restless. He went to Cutie's bed to see a box of counters, a red-veined stone, a bottle of bluebells, and more arranged artistically on a table nearby. He saw that his son had attempted to forget his dismissal by arranging the toys. He also saw that the emotional scar of the paternal rejection pained the boy deeper than the bodily scar left by the stick. Consequently, the father sobbed and kissed away the few drops of tears on his son's cheek, but leaving some of his.

This is in a nutshell Coventry Patmore's poem, 'The Toys'. The poem to me is an allegory of God-man relationship. We are like Cutie. In our hyper-active, materialistic rat race, we disobey godly commands and deviate into unchartered roads. God may reject us but soon will grow compassionate and forgive our trespasses.

After all, to err is human, and to forgive is divine.

God is like the unconditionally forgiving father of the prodigal son in the Bible. Remember the fallen woman, Mary, who was brought to the sage to be stoned to death according to the custom of the day. The sage's magic words—'Let him who hasn't sinned yet stone her first'—saved her, first from the cruel stones and second from her soiled past. The formula is forgive and redeem.

Once a monk, while visiting a monastery, was unable to resist the temptation for a rare book in the monastery library, and he stole it. Out in the market, he struck a deal with a book seller and agreed on a tentative price for the precious volume. As the book seller wanted a second opinion, he requested the monk to come the following day.

Interestingly, the book seller had the second opinion with the abbot (a great reader of many a book) from the very same monastery. The abbot had already known about the theft and the thief. 'How much could this book cost, sir? Fifty thousand?' the book seller enquired.
'Much more. Maybe a fortune,' the abbot said.

The next day the book seller told the eager monk the whole story. That was a moment of great realization for the monk. Instead of selling it, he took the book to the abbot.

The abbot said, 'When you borrowed the volume, I thought you should have it because you desired knowledge so much. Please keep it with you.'

The monk replied, 'No, sir. I would rather stay here and learn from you.'

The infinite, forgiving compassion in the abbot's words had touched him to the marrow. The irony, in particular in his words, 'borrowed' and 'desired' was inescapable.

Compassionate forgiving, not angry castigation, redeems. A royal pardon metamorphoses. A divine heart alone understands first, empathizes second, and forgives third. Kings, parents, and teachers possess such lofty hearts. All of us do.

10

To Be Better Livers

Once in 1986, Apa Wangda, a rich farmer in Bhutan aboard the small Druk Air Dornier flight to Calcutta, got angry with the air hostess, who had just reminded him to alight at the expiry of the fifty-minute flight. He hadn't enjoyed his first-ever experience of flying. He was asked to get down all too soon. He had just sat, settled himself down, and fastened the seat belt. That was all. Then he was shown the exit point by the pretty air hostess.

Apa Wangda, a student in the University of the Universe, had indeed known that for every ascent there was a descent. The illiterate Apa had also known that life and all its phenomena were cyclic. He who had seen sixty-five summers and winters had crossed on foot many mountains and valleys en route to Paro Phuentsholing, a long route covered today in five hours by car. But perhaps he didn't realize that his son, Alu Tempa, studied in school about carbon cycles and water cycles. This aerial ascent-descent cycle in the aircraft was too brief—the Apa learned a fresh lesson that day.

It is just and fair that all are cyclic on this oval earth. Our life on this oval earth is a relay race from the womb to the tomb. In that circular race, we cannot keep the relay baton with us; we just pass it to the next runner. That was why Alexander the Great desired that after death, his body be laid in such way that his empty hands were visible outside the coffin.

The relay race has four rounds. Imagine that one of the relay teams is led by Joe. When Joe finishes twenty-five years of this race as a human being, the referee asks him for the passing of the baton. But Joe, not having fully enjoyed the human race, asks the referee for one more round.

The referee replies, 'Sorry, all the rounds and time have been already distributed among various sentient beings. If you really want, borrow it from other creatures.'

He approaches a horse, who having led a burdensome life, readily gives Joe his share of the race. Thus, Joe continues a twenty-five-year horse life—getting a job, settling in life, and bringing up children. Joe, now at fifty, still thinks that the third round will be enjoyable, and he gets another twenty-five years, this time from a dog. Thus, the third round of our life is mostly guardianship, from the children's kids to their homes and properties. Man, even at seventy-five, dreams of a rosy tomorrow and borrows another twenty-five years from an owl. Man, at the dusk of his life, mostly leads an owlish stay on this oval earth—sans teeth, sans eyes, sans taste, sans everything, as Jaques said in *As You Like It*.

Only after the fourth round of the relay race do we, the Apa Wangdas pass our baton completely to our Alu Tempas. An awareness of this cyclic nature on this Sansara makes life more liveable and makes us better livers.

11

Tireless Striving

The famous British prime minister Winston Churchill ignited his army through his speech, popularly known as 'Blood, Sweat, and Tears.'

'I say to the House as I said to ministers who have joined this government, I have nothing to offer but blood, sweat and tears.'

His words moved a world; the British and the Allied forces, thus energized, won World War Two. Such was his indefatigable energy and optimism. The very same prime minister lost in the general elections after eleven weeks—but did it drain his hope? No. In four years' time, he ascended to the prime minister's office.

This saga of hard work and unyielding efforts has precedence in Abraham Lincoln, for an instance. In 1818 Lincoln's mother died; in 1832 he lost his job. Further setbacks comprised a business crash in1833, death of his sweetheart in 1835, a nomination defeat for Congress in 1843, and a defeat for the US Senate in 1854. At last, he was elected president of the country in 1860. His '14 defeats against 2 victories' makes the ratio seven to one.

It is now high time we asked ourselves, 'Are we the stuff that Churchill and Lincoln are made of?'

My grandpa had told me about a mother in our village. She was warned by the doctors during her pregnancy that her child was going to be crippled. An abortion was their advice, but it was not acceptable to her. A baby girl was born with only two fingers on each hand. 'Let some rich foreigners adopt it,' suggested her relatives. No. To her, the baby was the prettiest. She brought her up with love and care. She arranged for some piano lessons for the child. How can a four-fingered child manage the eighty-eight keys of the piano? But the mother persisted. Her relentless attempts at last bloomed: one day, her cute little angel played the first tune perfectly well! Soon, the child received prizes after prizes. Her mother shed profuse tears of joy.

The Scottish King Robert Bruce won his sixth battle after he was motivated by the repeated attempts of a spider. The spider was, in its web making, jumping from one side to the other of the cave where Bruce hid after he had fled from his fifth defeat.

Let's remember that the Pandavas in the *Mahabharatha* chose Lord Krishna—not his army—when given a choice between the two for the Kurukshetra battle. And the minority Pandavas won against the majority Kauravas when God (Lord Krishna) was their charioteer. But one's trust in the whole pantheon cannot save one in the absence of self-confidence, the Chicago-reputed Vivekananda teaches us. In a nutshell, tireless striving when you are confident in yourself and God will lead to sure success.

12

The Omnipresent Providence

Among the African tribes, there is a custom in which a young boy, upon reaching thirteen, will be sent blindfolded into a thick jungle, armed only with a bow and some arrows. The poor boy will not know that a trained tribal elder always accompanies him to see him through any eventualities. God's role is like the elder's. We are let out to fight our battle solo. Only then will our muscles develop.

Haven't you heard of a compassionate student in the biology lab who helped a pupa by rupturing its cocoon for the butterfly's easy escape? Though the teacher had warned the students against helping the cocooned pupa, the boy helped. A butterfly came out and struggled to fly, but it dropped to the ground and died. The struggle to come out of our miseries is a must, willed by God's infinite wisdom.

Once a man was shown by God, as on a film screen, a flashback of his life. Side by side, the picture also showed four footprints on the sands of time. When his most miserable phases in life flashed, there were only two footprints. The man sorrowfully asked God, 'See, why did you leave me on those needy times?'
God replied, 'My dear, on all those times, I carried you on my shoulders.'

The man felt ashamed of his distrust in God. Most of us resemble this man. Most, like the king in the fable, need to wear the happy man's shirt. The unhappy king—though surrounded by a host of faithful servants, steeped in wealth and luxury, and boasting the best army of the world—was prescribed a happy man's shirt. His people, in search of a happy man, almost gave up the quest. Then, they came across an extremely happy beggar, the only happy man they met. When demanded of his shirt, he said he had none.

The message was clear to the king. 'I went in search of a good pair of shoes until I met a man without feet.' As John Keats says, 'Here where we sit and hear each other groan . . .' It is sad that we forget to count our blessings. Marcus Aurelius says, 'We are what we think.'

13

Not for Greed, but for Need

A closed fist cannot receive. People say that our hearts are the size of our fists.

Emotional poverty starves our hearts, and then they could be small drawn and fist sized. This realization makes Rabindranath Tagore pray, 'Strike, strike at the root of penury in my heart.'

At the root of all poverty-eradication efforts of the world lies the Gandhian thought that the earth has enough for everyone's need but not for everyone's greed. The earth has enough for our material needs and is peopled with potentially loving and lovable fellows—enough and more for our emotional needs.

Akin to the Gandhian observation are the words of Henry John Kaiser: 'Give so long as God gives.' Kaiser was so poor in his childhood that he had to discontinue his studies, but sheer hard work led him to be the owner of the biggest cement factory in the United States.

A loving heart saves and redeems. 'You give so that you will be given,' says the sermon on the Mount in the Bible. Tagore also narrates a beautiful story. The king of kings (in *Gitanjali*) once stopped his chariot near a beggar. Expectant, the beggar stood before the king. The king asked him, 'You have nothing to give your king?' Perplexed, the beggar picked a grain from his bag and gave it to the king, thinking that His Majesty would sympathize with his poverty and reward him. In the evening, he was delighted to see a gold coin in his bag. It soon taught him a lesson, and he regretted that he had not given the entire grain to His Majesty. It is said that you will be measured by what you measure others with.

A similar story says that King Henry IV rewarded the poor man in the forest, who had given the disguised hunter-king an apple—all that he had for supper that evening. The Bible praises the widow's generosity (Luke 21:1-4). Jesus saw the crowd in the church putting money into the treasury. What struck him most was a widow's little money—two copper coins. That was all her earning, whereas the rich put only a small portion of their earnings. Thus she got God's blessings. The Romantic poet and philosopher Samuel Taylor Coleridge says, 'O Lady, we receive but what we give.'

Though the Coleridgean view has the profundity of subjective idealism, we must be content with the ethical consideration that our actions boomerang—love given assures love in return; wind sown results in storm reaped. Our mundane existence becomes beautiful when we practise this give-and-take policy.

The giving virtue, generosity, is one of the keys to contented life. In the act of giving, one touches open recipients hearts and eyes. They soon become one's unconditional supporters. Luke 6:38 says. 'Give and it will be given to you, a good measure pressed down, shaken together and running over, will be poured into your lap.'

14

The Steel Will Not Yield

Lines 31 and 70 of Lord Tennyson's poem 'Ulysses' say it all. The Trojan hero's indomitable spirit: 'To follow knowledge like a sinking star'. And later: 'To strive, to seek, to find and never to yield'.

It is this power of will that rewarded the hard-working frog in the milk tank. He and his friend, on one of their leisurely leaps, slipped into the tank. One gave up after a hundred odd jumps to get out of the milk tank. But the other went on jumping and at last felt something on his feet. He climbed on it and sprang out of the tank. What was that solid springboard? Churned-up butter. The Almighty recognized the industry—the unflagging effort unto the last.

The steel will make the winner leap. The Indian mountaineer Major H. P. S. Ahluwalia's steel enabled him to conquer Mount Everest in 1965 (he was just twenty-six then). But after having been crippled in the Indo-Pak War of the same year, his willpower, that invincible spirit of the Everest days, evaded him in his wheel chair. However, he regained his steel through prayers. His regained willpower said, 'Life is all about conquering the other summit—the Summit of the Mind.' Edmund Hillary's words must have motivated him: 'I'll come back to you [Mt. Everest]. You cannot grow taller but I can.'

John Milton, who despite his blindness wrote great poems, is an embodiment of steel will wrought in the smithy of disability. Sorrows in life are inevitable, but whether to manufacture steel or straw in the crucible of hardships is our choice. In fact, hardship should build hardihood. Socrates became a great seer by having been with his bellicose and shrewish wife, Xanthippe. He was once asked by Xenophon, 'Socrates, how is it that you don't practise what you preach—without educating your wife, you just live with her, who is the hardest to get along with?'

Socrates replied, 'Because horsemen don't get the most docile horses; but often they get the high-spirited ones, believing that if they can manage this kind, they will easily handle any other.'

The idea is that eyes awash with tears see better. Socrates thus has been a seer par excellence, to date.

15

Are You a Spade, a Sieve, or a Winnow?

Of the three neighbours in my village in India, Appunni is a spade, Martha is a sieve, and Achamma is a winnow. These are three forbidding metaphors, indeed (taken from Fr. Saji Pinarkayil).

While ploughing the field for paddy cultivation, Appunni ensures yearly that the boundary ridge between his and his neighbour's fields is pushed at least an inch out. Back in his grocery, he hides the extra packet of 'free' milk powder that the customer is entitled to, hushes up the offer of a cup and saucer as the bonus to a bigger buy. These 'free' bonuses he sells separately. Thus, Appunni has a 'pulling unto myself' urge: the spade complex. The amassing, possessing thirst has become a habit. The spade does not want to fight this habit. After all, you should call a spade a spade.

After her hectic morning chores, Martha relaxes. Children are off to school, and Adheham (her husband) is off in the field. She soon finds herself in the company of the gossip mongers, seated regularly in her verandah. A host of varied topics, often unconnected, is discussed passionately—from the prettier maidservant in the neighbourhood; the money-minting uncle, Chackochan; the handsome new principal, Mr. Shaji of the local school; the upcoming Perunnal (church festival) in the village; and the glittering saree Martha is going to wear.

Martha often concludes, 'My new saree is costly and is affectionately gifted by my husband. But the colour, I am sure, will fade soon. And . . . I don't think it is his real affection and feeling for me. After all, I have been telling him about it for ages, you know?'

On Chackochan she comments, 'Yes, yes, he does make money. But who knows how? One naturally has honest doubts . . .'

On the charm of Principal Shaji, she says, 'He is damn smart indeed . . . But mind you, outward appearances can be deceptive.'

Notice that Martha begins positively. But her tongue sifts them down, and what remains in her sieve are the unsavoury observations and bad conclusions. Martha is a sieve.

Achamma often opposes Martha. She qualifies the observation, 'Whether you, Martha, nagged on or not, at least he chose a good and costly saree. He could have easily bought you a cheap and gaudy one just to please you. I think that he has real feelings for you.'

Then she says, 'So long as he doesn't exploit people and doesn't harm us with his money, we had better be happy with Chackochan.' Achamma's words have a teacherly corrective edge over Martha's cynicism. Thus, Achamma is a winnow, letting off all the unwanted chaff but retaining the true grains of positive findings.

If this world of ours—where being negative is a fashion of late—were peopled with Achammas, life would be a heavenly experience. The Appunnis and Marthas would then be sidelined and at times even weeded out.

Be a winnow and be filled with the positive, winning energy.

16

The Pencil Superior to the Pen

A pencil defeats a pen in a charity competition, because the pencil sacrifices itself, like the burning candle, for the service of others. The pen simply flows out the ink with which it is fed. The pencil has unconditional fellow-feeling; the pen has just conditional service.

Once there lived two friends, a fallen leaf and a clod of soil. On one of their tours, a wind blew. Instantly the clod sat on the leaf. On their onward journey after the wind stopped, it rained. Then the leaf sat on the clod, protecting it like an umbrella. Thus they helped each other and reached their picnic spot. What beautiful fellow-feeling and mutual help!

On their post-picnic return journey, fate was cruel. It rained and the wind blew—together. The clod first sat on the leaf, but the rain dissolved it completely, and the leaf, thus unprotected, was blown away. So what? This was sublime martyrdom in the service of others. That is why it is said that there is no greater love than giving one's life for others. Jesus and many others did that. Though we ordinary mortals may not be as great as they were, we could at least be well mannered. Good manners are petty sacrifices.

A beautiful Aesop fable talks about a crippled traveller helping a blind one cross a very difficult patch of a path. The blind man carries the cripple; the cripple on his friend's shoulders guides him along the path. A great picture of mutual coexistence!

We must exist together. No one is rich enough to need no neighbours, as the Dutch proverb says. Each one of us wants to be wanted and needs to be needed. That is why Jesus advised us, 'Do unto others what you would be done by.' Buddhism teaches us not to do to others what you think will hurt you yourself. This is the kernel of fellow-feeling.

The classic example of unadulterated fellow-feeling is in the Good Samaritan in the Bible (Luke 10:25-37). The Samaritan nurses his ethnic enemy, a Jew, who was attacked and robbed on his way. There is merit in loving and nursing your enemy—not those who love you. The sweetness lies in one's greatness of—yes, it is nothing but greatness to love one's foe.

17

Compassion: Beyond Justice

Ap Tseten of Mongar, Bhutan, escaped grim depression and unwantedness only because of the postal runner—the poor Kota Sherab. Kota would bring with a smile the parcels and registered bank drafts to Ap Tseten, and he enquired after the old man's welfare in a ritual query: 'Apa, you are okay, aren't you?' The gifts and bank drafts came regularly from Apa's only daughter in the United States, who would never return to Mongar. Ap Tseten had practically no one else worth being called his. He stayed all alone, and the only comfort—a great relief indeed—was Kota Sherab's smiling face and kind words. Kota was the little oasis in Ap Tseten's desert.

Apa deposited his daughter's money in the bank, and in fact he is now a wealthy man. But the old man wanted not the money but human company. No wonder, upon his death, that Ap Tseten bequeathed his money to the oasis, the smiling Kota. Kota's smile cost him nothing, but it salvaged him from drowning poverty and misery.

Mercy and compassion are like the lifeboat when our ship is in threat. See how the sinner-woman, Mary Magdalena in the Bible, was saved from the angry crowd. To the Jewish custom, she should be stoned to death. The angry Jews asked Jesus, 'Shall we stone her?' Jesus's disarming words saved her: 'He who has not sinned yet can stone her first.' In a minute, the mob fury melted and no one was seen around. The rest is history: the sinner became a saint and left her sinful path.

She was touched because her suffering had touched the sage before. When others' sufferings touch the humanity in one, one may turn a saviour. See how Louis Pasteur became a historic saviour. Little Pasteur once happened to see a little boy being cauterized from the wound of a rabid dog's bite. When the hot iron sank into the poor boy's raw flesh, he writhed in pain. This painful sight cut Pasteur to the quick. He made a decision: 'I will discover a painless medicine against rabies.' This compassion-triggered inquiry led in 1885 to the invention of the anti-rabies drug.

Compassion begets empathy or sympathy and never apathy. Empathy is what we feel in the shoes of others—the exactness of feelings. Sympathy is kindness towards others' sufferings. Apathy is not feeling anything, the main cause of wars. Wars, ironically the barbarism of modern man, are still waged today because warmongers don't feel in their bodies and families what others feel. This numbness is the theme of the anti-war poet Wilfred Owen's poem 'Insensibility'.

Man, who is created in the image of God, is a wonderful creation, capable of infinite compassion. Hamlet exclaims, 'What a piece of work is a man! How noble in reason! How infinite in faculty.'

If a human heart beats 1,003,389 times a day without a feeling for others, if blood travels 270 kilometres per day with no kindly act for others, and if man utters 4,800 words a day on the average with no single happy phrase—then human life will draw a blank balance sheet in its conclusion, death. We who are such wonderful creations should be capable of angelic compassion and a genuine feeling for others—life's shock absorbers.

18

Guilt and Its Saving Merit

The so-called conscience bell troubles Arthur Dimmesdale in Nathaniel Hawthorne's classic *The Scarlet Letter*. The preacher has fathered Pearl with Hester Prynne. When Prynne has to face the humiliation of having to wear an 'A' on her dress for adultery, she refuses to reveal the identity of her partner. This tortures Arthur extremely. One day, unable to bear the guilt complex any more, he admits his mistake and dies.

A similar story is that of the torment which Dostoevsky's Raskolnikov undergoes till he reveals his double murder to the public. Guilt and its pangs are terrible. See the picture of tormented Macbeth, who sees daggers in the air! The portrayal of Lady Macbeth who washes her hands is admirable: 'Here's the smell of blood still; all the perfumes of Arabia will not sweeten this little hand.'

On the other side of the coin is the mercy of God. To err is human and to forgive is divine. The Bible talks about the prodigal son and the strayed sheep. The prodigal son, despite his extravagant life and waste of money, is pardoned by his ever-waiting father. Similarly, if one of the hundred sheep strays, the shepherd leaves all the ninety-nine sheep and goes in search of the single stray. Upon finding it, he celebrates the discovery of the lost sheep. In other words, God is like that father and shepherd, ready to pardon the erring human beings.

But the modern world has people who have frozen consciences so that they don't have the guilt complex. For example, E. M. Forster's protagonist, who receives the entire wealth of his father through the latter's will, is the owner of such a morbid conscience. There is, however, a condition: Give fifty thousand pounds to my sister. The man thinks it is okay. Against the huge wealth he has inherited, fifty thousand is a small amount. But gradually he thinks, "Even if I give only five thousand, my aunt will not know about it. For the will is with me." In the end, the greedy man decides to give nothing to his aunt at last.

Here is no conscience, no bell troubling modern man. This is an irremediable situation. Having at least the feeling of guilt is a good sign. That is why T. S. Eliot presents Jesus the redeemer as the tiger, juxtaposed against Jesus the lamb ('Gerontion').

A well-functioning conscience is a good asset; like the radar in the ship, it gives you the direction. Too much guilt feeling is bad. Instead, we should be ready to turn over a new leaf.

19

Are You God's Wife?

Little Chotu was a seven-year-old orphan in the big human ocean of Kolkota. Life had always been tough and rough to Chotu, having to compete with other orphans and beggars. In and around the Howrah railway station, on lucky days he would get one or two half-eaten lunches thrown away from the trains by overfed passengers. Such food he would gobble up with greatest relish before fellow beggars noticed him. On other lucky days, his begging progressed amidst scorns, slaps, and kicks, and the generous coins amounted to a handful, of which he would hide thirty or fifty Rupees in a cranny in the railway signpost. Somehow, the cranny was normally not noticed by others. And this occasional earning was the balance after giving his boss the daily compulsory hundred Rupees. Indeed, life to him was a tightrope walk.

One day, the hard-earned eighty Rupees of two days was missing from the cranny. Some thieves among the orphan beggars had taken it. Chotu felt devastated. He had treasured the money to buy a decent pair of shorts. He wept bitterly, sitting lost on the concrete base of the signpost, which housed his money. Not in a mood to beg or chase weaker beggars than him away from a train-dropped lunch pack, Chotu sat there for hours with an ebbing desire to live on. By mid-day, after the peak time of begging and earning, he felt terribly hungry. The awful prospect of facing his boss that evening empty-handed sent a wave of devilish fear down his spine. He stepped into the railway track, despair-blinded, daring the racing Rajdhani Express to approach.

Suddenly, a strong hand gently pulled him aside. He could not see what happened for a few minutes. The huge din and bustle and the confusing tumult expressed by the train was were blinding. When he opened his eyes, he saw he was lying in the lap of a middle-aged woman, who was smiling down at him with the world's kindest face. She said so many things unsaid, Chotu felt. Her kindness touched him to the marrow. He sobbed, and she wiped his tears. He asked her amid sobs, 'Are you . . . are you God's wife?'

'God's wife' has a hundred connotations here: Chotu's conceptualization of a male God; his feeling that wives partake in their husband's qualities; his notion that God is love and kindness; his feeling that women are a kinder lot than men. Yes, love is an emanation of godliness. But then, that love should be unconditional as God's wife's was. She had not known Chotu, but that ignorance was no bar for her stream of love to flow. Such unconditional love is unadulterated, for conditions adulterate love. Dostoevsky's Sonya's unconditional love for the murderer Raskolnikov redeems him. A teacher's pure love for his mischievous, disruptive child redeems it into a socially productive citizen. Jesus's unconditional love—which echoes in his words, 'Let he who has not sinned yet stone her first'—redeems the lost woman, Mary Magdelena. Mary turned to saintly ways, never to return. In other words, hers was a permanent change—the chemical change of love. That is the power of unconditional love. Every human heart craves to love and be loved; love given unsought will effect that chemical change. The change is possible only because it cares, it accepts, it never has to feel sorry.

Erich Segal defines love as never having to say 'I am sorry'. In the novel *Love Story*, rich Oliver Barrett is passionately in love with the poor Jennifer Cavelleri. The angry but wealthy father, Senior Oliver, cuts off all his links with his son. But the love thrives despite the marshy, thorny rejection from the ancestral home. First Oliver and then Jennifer come to know the terrible truth: that Jennifer is to die soon, having lately been a victim of leukaemia. The loving couple, already having a hard time making both ends meet, go for medical treatment. Oliver, buckling under unbearable financial pressure, knocks at his father's door for money. He got it, but it is not of much help. Oliver holds Jennifer tightly, and the young lady breathes her last breath. Hearing the news, Oliver Senior tells his son, 'I am sorry, my son.' The son said, 'Love is never having to say you are sorry.' In fact, he is repeating what Jennifer once told him when he was angry with her.

The loving father in the Bible never felt or said sorry. It was pure love that made the father wait for the prodigal son. It was the love of the red, excitable tulips that made the resigned Sylvia Plath accept at last the invitation to life, despite her initial adamant refusals to go back to it. It was the painter Berhman's love and devotion that gave life to the hopeless Johnsy in O'Henry's *The Last Leaf*. Put precisely, love is divine and redeems. Though saying sorry is good manners, non-judgemental and unconditional love takes away having to say one is sorry. God's wives are like that—they never say sorry; they are proactive for the sake of just love.

20

My Shortness Is My Tallness

The title above is paradoxical, shortness equated with its opposite. Let's tame the paradox.

Who should wish first, the teacher or the student when they meet? Usually the student, but what if the student avoids or evades the teacher? What if the teacher wished the evading student? It would definitely have a double effect. One, the student would readily wish the teacher back. Two, the student would henceforth gain the confidence and the need-awareness (a great value) to wish others without hesitation.

There is no short or tall, big or small in wishing others. Wishing another human being is desiring good days for the fellow. Thus, there is no hierarchy or position in this gesture except the beautiful designation: human. The human designation is the guarantor of parity—all have the divine spark in them. It is this divinity that we bow to wish when we greet a human being.

The great Shankaracharya of India once learned the lesson of human equality from a so-called low-caste man. The latter was asked by the forerunner to give way to the acharya on a public road. The low-born protested, 'Should the God in me give way to the god in the acharya?' The sage was instantly ignited with the eternal verity called universal human equality. Since then the acharya has crusaded against discriminations of all sorts.

Human equality is at the heart of the Orwellian sarcasm of 'All . . . are equal, but some . . . are more equal.' Of course, some achieve the unmathematical 'more equality', or superiority, through their merit. The father, for example, is superior to his little son on many accounts—the merit of having weathered many summers, winters, men, and manners. But he bends down and ties the shoelace of his son. Still, the son accepts his father's tallness despite the temporary shortness at lace tying. In fact, it is this paternal shortness that is indisputably the tallness.

For another example, the tallness of the ocean is its vastness. Still, it does not swell at the thought of taking in all river waters. The tallest of all, the sun, shines with exemplary eternal punctuality without taking pride that all exist just because of him. This is the shortness of the mighty ocean and the lofty sun. Thus, that one's shortness is one's tallness is an inalienable truth of nature. So is it in our lives.

The towering Jesus washed the leg of his disciples, advising them, 'He who is the leader should be the servant' (Luke 22, 24). 'Minister' literally means 'servant'. It is common knowledge that the branches having more fruits bend low—but they are strong and flexible. Strength and agility make something tough. Wealth of knowledge and range of performance make one humanly tall and humble.

How do we get these merits, range of knowledge and performance? Ambition, industry, and experience (AIE) form the triple gem for merit. In fact, ambition flows to industry, which leads to experience. Experience is, to quote the irresistible Tennysonian metaphor,

> an arch wherethro'
> Gleams that untravell'd world whose margin fades
> For ever and for ever when I move.

It is implied here that the more you know (taller), the humbler you become (shorter). Didn't the great Isaac Newton compare himself to a little boy with just a few stones and shells on the seashore? The humbling effect of the awareness of the vast, unexplored sea is the product of knowing the sea a little. We hail Newton's shortness as his tallness.

There are just two ways to be tall: one, by being tall oneself; two, by lowering others. Some adopt the second method, proclaiming thereby that they are in fact short. Perhaps their shortness would not have been noticed if they had remained what they were.

21

Scars of Anger

An impatient mother once took her teenage son to a master. Her request was to help the boy to overcome his short temper. 'Why, you could help him, couldn't you?' the man asked.

'No, sir. I myself need to control my temper.'

'Well! Please give me a month's time. I am training myself to master my emotions.'

Let's salute the mother's honesty and more so the master's.

After a month, the boy appeared at the master's and was asked to fix a nail on a white wall every time he burst out in anger. Meanwhile, the master trained the boy in the art of self-control and of sweet words. It took six months of rigorous practice for the adolescent to be a self-controlled lad. Then the master asked him to remove a nail off the wall every time he responded to people and situations coolly and self-composed. When he removed all the nails, the master gave him the following message.

> It's good that you cleared the wall of all nails. But, look, the wall has become dirty. The scars and wounds of the nails are still left unremoved. Even after our apology or reconciliation, the scars remain. That's why ancient wisdom tells us that the joint—whether refastened or welded with utmost skill—will still bulge. So the best thing is to see that our short temper does not snap the cord of friendship.

This is possible only if we have positive eyes and a positive tongue. Positive eyes make us love all around us, and a positive tongue makes all around us love us. What a wonderful world will it be when we love all and all love us! This is the magic of tolerance and sweet words.

Lord Buddha advises us to avoid bad words and angry utterances as life lovers avoid poison. It is possible that we get angry in our daily business of life. But as Winston Churchill quips, nobody gets stomach problems because of swallowing bad words. As prince Hamlet felt, this world is like an unweeded garden. We are likely to have unpleasant brushes with sharp weeds around us. Human inclination to vices is said to be natural and unchangeable; one cannot change the properties of Plutonium, said Einstein.

What then is the way out? Develop tolerance and the art of tactful talk. Once an atheist knocked at the door of Abram, the great patriarch of the Old Testament. (Remember that he was ready when so commanded by God even to kill his only child; that too born in old age after years of waiting) As he opened the door, the tired traveller asked him for a night's shelter. Abram asked him, 'Do you believe in God?'

'No, I am an atheist,' replied the traveller.

'Off you go.' Abram was trembling with anger.

That night, God reprimanded Abram in his dream: 'I have tolerated this man for fifty years. You could not, just for a night?'

That was the divine command: *unconditional tolerance*. Shylock's vehement plea for tolerance seems a fitting conclusion to this piece:

> Hath not a Jew eyes? . . . If you prick us, do we not bleed?
> If you tickle us, do we not laugh? If you poison us, do we not die?

22

Pray to Stay

Mr. Chadurman Rai, in a far-away Indian village, had the habit of talking to his goods carrier—a brown, handsome horse. Every week they would tread the rugged path of thirty kilometres, the Rai transports carrying blankets, sweaters, and jackets to the next town for sale. On these lonely trips, Mr. Rai talked about his personal problems to the horse. His horse nodded and swayed its head as if in response. Having a keen listener is a blessing.

'Why not talk to the God in my heart?' Mr. Rai's interest was sudden. So he started the talk, convinced that God was listening to him and giving him bits and pieces of advice. Such talks became a routine, and Mr. Rai found a great source of inner strength and motivation from this interior dialogue.

This soul-born dialogue is prayer—that between the self and the omniscient, the created and the creator. Prayer is an exercise of inner energy generation on one condition. We should have 100 per cent trust in the Almighty. Even a mustard-seed belief in God enables one to command a hill to move, it has been said. That is the magical power of undoubting belief.

Look at children, who have total trust in their parents. "My father can defeat an elephant" is child-like confidence. Such a confidence and trust in our divine father is the prerequisite of effective prayers. We, the confident children of his, thus would start the day praying. That's why Gandhi advises us, 'Let your prayer be the lock to the dusk and the key to the dawn.'

But we are mostly doubting Thomases. As Matthew Arnold sings, we are vague half-believers of our casual creeds. We are like Samuel Beckett's Estragon and Vladimir, who in half-belief wait for Godot and never meet him. We fail to realize that a shopping list of our needs in our prayers is not 'the thing'. Rather, it is the absolute trust in the Most High that takes care of all the rest.

'If you, O God, let me score distinction in my examinations, I will offer you a hundred butter lamps or light a hundred candles.' Thus often goes our prayer. We thus set conditions—that too with God. How baseless! How unreasonable! Some others give up praying, saying God is a sadist who, instead of granting our prayers, unleashes hardships on us. We fail to realize that God, in his infinite wisdom, teaches us how to fish rather than give us the fish. The learning of fishing is often misinterpreted as hardship. But mind you, no pain, no gain.

There is a reassurance: he who knocks will be opened too; she who searches will find. Heart-born prayers are the knocks and searches that one must make. Mr. Rai knew untaught the joys of quiet prayers and then discovered the springs of inner energy. He prayed innocently and he stayed firmly.

23

Passionate Civil Servants

Socrates commanded, 'Come to me when you want knowledge as much as you wanted air a while ago.' The listener was a young man who was lifted out of water after having been dunked into it for a couple of breaths. The young man had come to the Greek teacher after a fashion for knowledge. Socrates saw through his passionlessness for knowledge. Hence the stupendous Socratic practical wisdom.

The passion that Socrates sought was akin to, but not the same as, Archimedes's passion when he suddenly floated upon the long sought-after truth about buoyancy. None would forget his naked passion as he ran along the streets, shouting 'Eureka'. The Eureka passion was born when the principle of buoyancy came to him in a bathtub!

Archimedes also discovered the combustibility of a burning object to set afire another. Anything that burns pulls us—even the most casual—to it. That is the simple sequence:

Burn yourself ⎯⎯⎯⎯⎯➤ Burn others

The sequence worked with my cousin (a class IX undergraduate) and his dad (a class II drop-out). The undergraduate goes to his father with a math problem in solids. The quivering, withered hands of the old peasant picks up an unshapely stone from his ill-defined courtyard; draws some lines on it with a colour stone (that too from the courtyard), explains to him, asks him questions, and reinforces his son's responses. And there my cousin stands in the courtyard, glowing with understanding, seeing his uneducated, untrained father performing far better than his trained math teacher at school.

My uncle uses a lot of teaching aids which are improvised. He uses skills such as prompting, probing, reinforcing, and so on—not because he is trained but because he, the uneducated farmer, is burning with the passion of the content.

The old man, a passionate lover albeit uneducated or even illiterate, effectively implants his love-mantra in his beloved's heart. That heart never forgets the thrill; the amorous exhilaration lives there unto the last.

The common denominator—the only one—is passion.

To live up to high levels of passion, we need passionate civil servants. Some truly are, we can boast legitimately. Not to mince words, however, we should call a spade a spade. Some come to office late and leave it early; some find themselves in the canteens more than in the offices; some while away their time with computers. A few of our teachers, plagued by passionlessness, stay on their teaching berths as liabilities to the profession Malvolio-like (after Shakespeare's <u>Twelfth Night</u>), as the nobility of the profession is thrust upon them.

The zest for one's job is best exemplified by the third mason involved in the construction of St. Paul's cathedral in London. To the famous architect of the cathedral, Sir Christopher Wren in disguise, the three masons in work said the same thing differently. The first said, "I'm working on a stone." The second said, "I'm constructing a wall." And the third said, "I'm helping build the most magnificent cathedral in the world, designed by the famous Christopher Wren."

24

Ad hocism Is a Wet Blanket on Performance

Little Johnsy had been inexplicably excited since her parents announced a possible trip to her uncle's, soon after her mid-term exams. But most often, excitements die young. In the morning of the day of the proposed trip, Johnsy's mother had to be rushed to hospital for severe headaches and vomiting. The trip thus stood boringly cancelled. Such an unwelcome ad hoc sickness! Johnsy cursed the sickness with all the abusive vocabulary she had recently picked up. (Sometimes your word bank feels so poor!) God-willed ad hocism. Man can only propose; God then will dispose.

Another ad hocism: Level III Kate said to me, 'Sir, Mr. Malcolm coming; paper picking; principal telling . . .' Though I felt excited at the cute Katean progress of the progressive tense without the auxiliary, the ad hocism she announced blew out the earnestly burning candle of poetry discussion. In this ad hocism, the man (me, the lesson-planned teacher) proposed, but another body of men (the school inspectorate) or the principal disposed. Thus it is man-made, unlike the God-willed ad hocism above.

Suddenly, my friend, a doubting Thomas, cut in. 'The inspectors should come unannounced. Also, if you're planned, why worry?'

'My worry is not the inspectors' visit; it is the interruption of my thrilling poetry lesson. Ad hoc announcements arrest me and my students from reaching the learning climax—those beautiful moments of teaching-learning. Once interrupted, recreating the same tempo, readiness, and receptivity in your performance is near-impossible.'

True, an ad hoc earthquake or a fire accident may interrupt us, but they are God-willed, not man-willed. The child has made enviable progress in leaps and bounds since I knew her. But ad hocism has done well too. One wishes things could be otherwise.

We cannot eliminate ad hocism from our midst; this is common knowledge. But we can reduce its instances. If we don't, it will act as a wet blanket on the ignited performance of a civil servant. An unannounced meeting, that meeting's prolonging beyond reasonable limits, a whimsical football match, an enforced visit, an unprepared-for professional enhancement programme abroad, a hurriedly arranged supervision and monitoring trip—these are but a few examples of what we should streamline.

On another front, 'The page cannot be displayed' on the computer screen after thirty minutes or so of waiting for vital information for one's work and profession is ad hocism that we can have control over and streamline more often than not. Are the unexpected though frequent power failures when an important file is getting downloaded a professional coitus interruptus or a curse?

Which of the above can have human solutions? Are we happy to fall into the complacency groove, shrugging the shoulders and saying, 'Can't help'? The more controllable (not ad hoc) most situations are, the more brushed up and lustrous will our professionalism be. We 'shine in use', or else we 'rust unburnished', to borrow from Lord Tennyson. Shining work force is a pride to the nation, rusting servants its liabilities.

25

Listen, Just Listen: Half of the Delinquencies Melt!

In class VIII my first period was a lesson in chemistry. In fact, chemistry was thrust on me as greatness on Shakespeare's Malvolio, extra to my English. That day, I was confident with balancing of equations because I had had ample help from a veteran chemistry teacher.

But as I neared the classroom, I saw four girls and a couple of boys standing outside. I asked them why. 'Stinking, sir, stinking,' some said half in anger and half in revulsion, whereas two of the girls evaded my question.

A classroom stinking? In baffled wonder I stood there and waited. The academic space called the classroom should be wafting the fragrance of knowledge and skills!
'Sir, our Jerome has vomited . . . He is drunk,' one of the evader-girls informed me in a volley of words, drenched in disgust.

Though I could not believe my ears, I entered the classroom and saw a huddle of Jerome sound asleep at his desk, his morning contribution, the vomit, lying at his feet in a puddle. Yes, the room did stink.

I asked Jim, the strongest of the boys, to carry Jerome to the hostel. He did, and we soon cleaned the room. The rest of my students—a manageable eleven of them—actively washed and mopped. After all, they excelled in non-academic exercises, though they struggled in studies.

I thought I would teach my confident balancing of equations. But then, the other evader-girl could not control herself and said, 'Sir, these boys should not drink, right?' A sweeping generalization, indeed, and a legitimate moral anguish!

She went on at some length on the sacrilege that Jerome had committed. I listened with fond curiosity and interest in her honest, innocent outburst as a grandpa would listen to his grandchild's moral outrage.

Then, I talked on the pros and cons of drinking, citing examples of accidents and family wreckages precipitated by drinking. I assured them that Jerome's case would be discussed in a staff meeting, and due action would be taken. In a minute, the bell rang and I did not balance.

As our principal had been away, the officiating principal called a staff meeting, in which Jerome was suspended from the school for a week. Therefore, an unusual assembly was held, which Jerome—now apparently sober—attended.

No sooner was his suspension announced than Jerome (one of the tallest of the lot) shouted from behind, 'You hopeless teachers, why a suspension? What did I do?'

The bewildered staff dismissed the assembly. Jerome went on and on with his rabid ranting among the scattered students. Soon a core group of teachers was formed as counsellors. Each of them listened to Jerome in turn. (It is not a secret that some of them coaxed, advised, and threatened too.) At last he relented and came up with a long apology letter, with misspellings, run-ons, fragments, whimsical articles, and tense shifts.

The novice teacher in me noticed then the impact of listening and counselling; he who came as lion was humbled as a lamb. That incident was a crucible of transformation for Jerome; today he is a gem of a responsible citizen. His teachers' patient listening to his soul and his nurture was like a soothing shower on the parched soil. That was the miraculous healing touch. Listen in empathy, not sympathy; it works wonders.

But have we the luxury of time? Haven't we got misplaced priorities that rob our time? Much of our mindset about discipline is rooted in the philosophy of the cane. Many of us are sadistic disciplinarians. In the words of the Indian writer R. K. Narayan:

> I used to think that one's guru was born clutching a cane in his right hand while the left held a pinch of snuff between the thumb and forefinger. He took a deep inhalation before proceeding to flick the cane on whatever portion of myself was available for the purpose. I really had no idea what I was expected to do or not do to avoid it. I could never imagine that a simple error of calculation in addition, subtraction or multiplication (I never knew which) would drive anyone hysterical.

26

Richard's Knowing Smile on Value Sermons

Richard, at level IX, gave a knowing smile and told me, 'Sir, these are ideals easier preached than practised.' Richard's confidence quotient was high, his frankness above average. As his value education teacher, I liked both. His knowing smile was gnawing at my conviction that smuggling (the topic of the just-concluded lesson) was an evil when he elaborated, 'Sir, my uncle is a respected rich man in the village; he smuggles and sells. He is doing absolutely normal.'

This bygone encounter with Richard's honesty surfaced recently in my mind when I read about the concerns of 'Whither our youth?' Richard is like the hospitalized young boy in Bimal Mitra's 1912 novel *The Twentieth Century*. He is hospitalized because he named to the principal the boy who had shouted in the class.

The sobbing mother at his hospital bed reproves him for his dangerous honesty. 'You were the only honest boy of the 35 students in the class?—so you got the reward: a bloody, bandaged head!' (The identified boy had stoned him on their way home.) Confusing values from the very mother who repeatedly advises him to be honest, whatever the odds! The same mama who cites anecdotes from the Harischandra tales!

Richard had, however, outlived such confusions. In the microcosm of the school, Richard had been listening to sermons and discussions (more the former) on values such as honesty, fair business, selfless devotion, and the like. He stepped outside into the macrocosm and confronted people who were world-wise, pragmatic, and utilitarian. They were successful, hailed as smart. No wonder Richard had started sitting in the value education classes with a knowing smile. The latter is an armour against all sermons. He told success stories of uncles who are not straightforward, irresistible triumph tales of aunties who are a bit sly, and slightly deviant cousins having good times in life from parallel inculcation.

Parallel Inculcation

Indeed, the inculcation of values at home is effective and sublime, that at school good but often ritualistic. The nutrients absorbed from the home soil help, but home has no control over the rains, the hailstorms, or the acid rains. At least some of the TV channels belong to the latter group. They often prove as stronger influences on tender minds than the home and school inculcations. Even home trends are changing. Mothers who once served food with overwhelming love and native dutifulness see today such services as being a servant. Fathers who once treasured the sweat-pickled toil today find shortcuts to achievements. No wonder the youth stray in the absence of potent role models. E. M. Forster stresses that culture and values are to be role-modelled, not prescribed or sermonized.

27

Cost Effectiveness versus Mediocrity

Tom, a level X student, listened to his math madam's volley of warnings in cool indifference: 'Tom, you know Math is a major subject. You fail in Math; you fail in many things. So be serious. Bring your homework regularly.' His math madam (which later shrunk into 'mad madam' in students' parlance) paused to breathe in some air. Then on she went. 'You also know that homework is a part of the continuous assessment, and your CA is 20 per cent.'

Envying the unmathematical sparrow whistling by, Tom replied, 'Don't worry, ma'am. Of the forty-two students in my class, at least thirty-eight will pass this year. Then, I'll pass, For, I have maintained the thirty-second or thirty-third position through the year.'

Tom's is an echo of the whole class's understanding. To the question, 'How do you know thirty-eight students will pass?' Tom replies, 'This has been happening through the years—about 90 per cent of students pass yearly. I'm not so bad as to belong to the 10 per cent remaining, I know.'

Most of our little Johns, Teresas, Biancas, and Emilys don't worry about major and minor subjects, or about the role of continuous assessment. Having tasted the sweetness of easy passing, they nestle snugly in the cushion of mediocrity.

Is mediocrity the deformed child of cost effectiveness? Cost effectiveness is a good administrative safety belt, if only enabling conditions prevail. In the absence of the latter, the belt either loosens, cracks, or snaps.

No, the machine should not come to a grinding halt for the loose belt! So let's lavish CA marks; let's make our subject bar graphs comfortably tall enough to ward off explanations. Let's lower the cut-off percentage to take in more candidates to fully utilize the infrastructure and facilities (in the way of the shop keeper lowering the price of a commodity upon the customer's apparent lack of interest in it). Such exercises of playing it safe and of the market ploy engender mediocrity.

The poet who sang, 'If I were a cobbler I'd make it my pride / The best of all cobblers to be / If I were a tinker, no tinker beside / Should mend an old kettle like me,' is an enemy of mediocrity. Dr. Martin Luther King Jr.'s words, 'If a man is called to be a street sweeper, he should sweep streets as Michelangelo painted or Beethoven composed music or Shakespeare poetry' is the gospel of 'excellence', the antonym of 'mediocrity'.

It is high time our schools studied the causes of mediocrity among its Toms, Johns, Teresas, Biancas, and Emilys. One cause obviously is what Shakespeare said: 'Light winning makes the fruit light'. If our kids win promotion lightly, they will rate the 'passing' lightly. If the pupa is helped to come out of its cocoon, the butterfly will fly a little and drop dead. The recent Commonwealth Games and Asian Games testify that athletes, when challenged, break world records. After all, kites soar not with the wind but against the wind.

One force that pulls the kite down is the parochial goal some set for education: passing the examinations and getting a job. Churned from the cost-effectiveness philosophy, this goal pins down the students and teachers, unless highly professional, to mediocrity. The 'pass the exam' craze often generates human copiers of textbooks and teachers' notes. We have examples of doctors, who once had topped the rank lists, sit puzzled at more aggressive diseases and more complex patients—whose symptoms and remedies were not there in the books they had studied by heart.

The drive here is not for excellence. We thus run the risk of producing a generation of youngsters who believe in no dreams except those of money making. Louis Pasteur had dreams. Thank God money wasn't there in his dreams of making an anti-rabies vaccine. And Pasteur excelled. Marie Curie excelled. Such great dreamers of the worlds were not driven by the money motive. That some of them became rich was just an unplanned by-product of their excellence. Excellence is multiple times cost effectiveness.

A paradox? Yes. Excellence is the antonym of mediocrity. Mediocrity is often the product of cost effectiveness. Paradoxically, excellence is many fold cost effectiveness.

Cost effectiveness is a genuine parental concern—every pound invested is well used and should yield rich dividends. That's fine. But a ruthless enforcement of this philosophy with much less concern about the enabling conditions at the operational levels often results in mediocrity. Here, the product becomes the sole concern, not the process. No wonder our children don't learn—they are forced to learn. They celebrate mediocrity whereas some 0.5-1.0 per cent in the class celebrate perspiration. The Toms thus have a knowing smile on their 'mad madam' warnings.

28

Students' Learned Helplessness in Writing

Jamie Crawford, a level X student, is 'hopeless' in writing essays. The hopelessness comprises as poverty of ideas, loose organization, incoherence, ill-defined topic sentences, and—much to the teachers' chagrin—the failure to belong. His essays, in the pedagogic jargon, evades classification— argumentative, expository, narrative, and you name it . . . 'My God, they just don't belong,' is something in the fashion of O'Neill's *The Hairy Ape*.

Such Crawfordean hopelessness, the seasoned teaching fraternity admits, is a frequent stone in the otherwise delicious curry of teaching English. Highly recommended remedies from within and without the country have been tried—writing portfolio, writers' workshop, relay writing, peer editing, and so on. Despite these remedies, many of our Crawfords are still substandard writers. The teacher's label 'hopeless' sticks and sinks, and the Crawfords continue to be such even in tertiary institutes once sneaked in.

I may be allowed to call this writing handicap 'learned helplessness'. Once when Crawford was still in class X, I chanced to read a pretty long love letter he had meant for his girlfriend, Jennifer. Head over heels in love with Jennifer for a month, Chencho had struggled hard to clear a misunderstanding that had so mischievously crept into her head. But the struggle was in vain, and Jennifer was not convinced. Crawford sat down, and his sorrow and helplessness sat down with him. So did his undiluted passion for Jennifer from his pining heart. And they together wrote that wonderful piece. It's Crawford—his heart, soul, brain, self-image, and esteem—that wrote it. "I am large; I contain multitudes," as Whitman sang. A Whitmanesque charm his love letter had, indeed.

It had marvellous richness of ideas, cogent argumentation and silky persuasion, coherent presentation, and bull's-eye–hitting quotes. A wave of exhilaration ran down my spine as I read it. The composition was immaculate except for some jarring grammar slips, which hardly interfered with its irresistible communication.

Crawford's is an interesting case study. He is 'hopeless' in a typical classroom academic writing but superb (at least to me) in one of his personal writings. When he writes to Jennifer, he is not worried about the hierarchy of the process of writing; he is not in the least bothered about the topic sentences in each paragraph; never does coherence distract his flow. He just does not know to which subgenre his essay belongs. But still, his finished product shows all of them.

Then what was the big motive force, the great enabling factor when he wrote? He was passionate; he targeted a 100 per cent persuasion of Jennifer; his audience was concrete. Crawford's inability for academic writing was learned helplessness. His teacher with good intentions taught him the chemistry of writing, the philosophy of the audience, the tone and coherence, and at last the taxonomy of the genre essay. He lost his way in this academic jungle, and he developed a belief in his inability to write a well-knit essay; he thought he did not belong.

Can we let our students love what they write? Let them have before them a concrete audience. Let not the high-sounding jargons of academic writing distract them. Academic writing then will become a hot cake and a cup of welcome tea to our students. Let them belong, unlike O'Neill's Yank.

A father tells his son, 'Dear son, Becky is a nice girl. I like her. Why don't you marry her?' The son obliges out of filial duty. Before long, their marriage sails in rough waters.

29

A Good Teacher Is Doubly Romantic

Once I bit a stone in the curry of my friend, Mr. John T.V. Mr. John had said, 'Teaching is the most noblest profession.'

'How dare he attempt the Shakespearean license of the double superlative?' I fumed. The rather pedantic grammar precision in me was ruffled. But he stuck to his guns and said a single superlative was too weak to capture the holiness and nobility of the teacher's office—too convincing a point.

School is a temple, and the teachers there are priests and priestesses. I agree to the Kothari Commission on Indian Education (1964-66) that the destiny of a nation is being shaped in her classrooms. Education equips the students with personal, moral, and national qualities. Thus, teaching is very different, holier, and more taxing than any other professions.

Any Tom, Dick, or Harry cannot become a teacher. But often this happens, and that is the biggest tragedy of modern times. Only a Rogerian personality can become a teacher. It thus follows that teacher education normally cannot beget this teacher personality, but it can help in its blooming. The Rogerian personality is made up of congruence in character, unconditional acceptance of the pupil and empathy. Thus, a teacher is often born, not made. The supreme teachers the world has ever seen—Socrates, Lord Buddha, Jesus, and Gandhi, to mention but a few—are testimonies to this fact.

These gurus were doubly romantic—they were romantic with their teachings and were romantic with the taught. Being romantic with the subject and with the students—these twin romances sum up guruhood. All teacher qualities one can think of are just their offshoots.

Dating with the Subject

Romance with one's subject makes one date with, say, poetry, mathematics, history, and geography. One will then have the Eureka passion and the insatiable thirst to share it with others, to shout to the world the beauty of one's beloved. One who is burning with the content will have a natural, insatiable desire to share it with his or her students. Thus instructional methodology smoothly follows or flows, even when untrained. I remember my uneducated uncle having used a variety of improvised teaching aids (mostly collected from our backyard; once the rice box in our kitchen) to drive home how he got the solution to some math problems which my cousin had put forward to him. Was my uncle trained? He hardly reached level III and dropped out. But my cousin learned more math from him than any of his trained schoolteachers.

The simple truth is, every human being, while burning with the content and an immaculate love of the disciple—the Rogerian personality—naturally and effectively teaches. My uncle passionately loved math and his son. The narrator in Chetan Bhagat's *The Three Mistakes of My Life* loved math and his student, Vidya, despite her comment: 'Between an electric shock or a Maths test, I will choose the former.'

Or think of an amorous lover. He is immensely capable of delivering his messages to his beloved, but not because he has been trained. And these messages the receiver remembers throughout life. The point is that every human heart has a teacher in it. Pump in content; the lurking teacher will rear its head out of the gurgling hot spring of the content.

The Teacher Being Romantic with the Student

Here the shoe pinches when the phrase is parochially interpreted. The sunflower is in romance with the sun. In *Titanic*, Jack Dawson is in love with sketching Rose Bukater nude. Nobody sees any erotic intentions in the sunflower or in the artist in DiCaprio or in my uncle the peasant-teacher. Highly professional teachers' love for their disciples belong to the realm of agape, not Eros. Agape is fatherly love, uncontaminated by the life instinct of the erotic Eros. The guru, when doubly romantic, is not afflicted or diverted by any other considerations, including sexual love. Just as the great archer in the *Mahabharata* saw nothing else except the neck of the bird to be shot at, a romantic teacher sees only his subject and his students. In this case the shoe does not pinch at all.

These twin romances form the teacher-quality, be it in senior teachers or a novices. You name any other traits desired in teachers or the salient elements in the teachers' code of conduct. They are there in the duo aforesaid. Such a teacher is equipped with tact and affection, which Bertrand Russell says can replace school rules, however wisely conceived.

Tact and affection help the teacher to affect the ownership of learning by students. The content-ignited, affectionate, self-motivated teacher tactfully facilitates learning and self-discovery by students. No wonder the Buddhist kaon asks us to kill the Buddha (teacher) if we meet one on the road. It is this killing—that is, withdrawal of the inspiring teacher—that makes pupils the owners of their learning. Owners are proud preservers and practitioners. The ultimate success of education lies here, in preserving and practising what is learned.

It leads to a foregone conclusion: we reward and preserve romantic teachers; we sift out potentially unromantic teacher candidates. Let's be reminded of the Kothari advice: our classrooms are the crucibles of the country's future, and teachers are the engineers, next in importance to none.

30

Word Grilling

Add an's' to 'Word', and it becomes 'sword'. And's' stands for 'severe'. No wonder my daughter dreaded the so-called counselling by her school counsellors in India. She said it was not counselling; rather, it was grilling. I would use the Indian columnist Jug Suraiya's statement, 'Word is a four-letter word' to apply to such grilling sessions. And she preferred corporal punishment to such word grilling. I bet she is one of the very many who would hold such preferences.

Does their preference warrant a reversion in our schools to the gospel of the cane—'Spare the rod and spoil the child'? Perhaps vehemently yes. Not that the cane, or for that matter R. K. Narayan's glorified birch, is pedagogically virtuous, but it is a lesser evil than grilling.

Whereas grilling deeply cuts the mind and soul, the cane at worst cuts deep only the skin and muscles. A modicum of common sense tells us that touching others' person without their consent is an offence, a social taboo whatsoever the reason. It's brute forcing, not human courtesy. Are teachers, the custodians and inculcators of courtesy and manners, exempt from that basic courtesy?

On the other side of the coin, I see the etching of a story of one Ganashyam Giri. Gane (my pet name for him) in level VIII is a devoted truant. Much of the teachers' efforts to lure him to the school fail. The concerned class teacher asks Gane's brother, an old friend of the teacher's, to persuade the little boy to continue his studies. The senior brother shrugs his shoulders and says he is helpless, having counselled the boy for a week.

One day, the teacher is served a cup of tea by Gane in a popular hotel in the town. The teacher could not believe his eyes. Upon the mildest inquiry, Gane informs his teacher that he is very happy as a supplier in the hotel. 'The school . . . ?' Gane left his statement incomplete.

A couple of sips later, the teacher tells him, 'It's okay, Gane. It's good that you are doing what you like. However, don't you think that if you continue your schooling, you might get a better job?'

"No, sir. Somehow I like this job. I am determined to continue here.'

'Well!' the teacher said. 'Gane, it's so important and good that you like the work. But you should take the transfer certificate from the school. You know, the TC will be useful in your future. You are so young, and you could look for other jobs too. So, please come to the school for that; I'll help you. Okay?'

'Okay, sir, I shall come.'

In school the following day, the teacher welcomes Gane with a lot of warmth and tenderness. He says, 'Gane, see how happy the students are? They are running around and playing. Don't you now feel that you like the school?'

"Sorry, sir . . . Please give me the TC.'

'Gane, your TC has been prepared, and you can take it. But before that, why don't you go to your class, meet your friends, and say bye to them?'

'Yes, sir, I'll do it.'

Soon, both of them are in the classroom. The teacher tells the class, 'Dear boys and girls, your friend Gane is leaving the school. Let's wish him all the best. But don't you want him to be with you? Won't you be missing him?'

'Yes, sir, we'll be missing him,' came the thunderous chorus. 'We want him . . . we want our Gane with us, sir.'

Turning to Gane, still downcast, the teacher said, 'See, Gane, how much your friends love you, how much we teachers love you? Now, tell me: you still want to take your TC? Why don't you please stay with us?'

'Very sorry, sir. I must go. Please help me get the TC.'

The teacher went and bolted the door from inside. He then stormed back and hit Gane, asking, 'You still want to go? Giving a damn to our care and request . . . ?' Gane, evading the blows, is heard screaming, 'Sir, I'll not go . . . I'll stay back and study, sir, please . . .'

Gane, thus battered black and blue, resumes his schooling. (The last I heard, Gane topped levels X and XII results!)

Later in the staffroom, Gane's teacher smirks and formulates what has become a quotable quote: 'Where Western counselling fails, Eastern counselling works.'

Pat says, 'No student will ever dare before you.'

Another adds, 'Primitive behaviour needs primitive punishment.'

A third quips, 'Physical punishment is a necessary preamble to the child's constitution.'

My daughter and her co-sufferers must have meant that such quick shock treatments as Gane got are far better than the slow, protracted verbal tortures of 'advising'.

Here's the rub. Most often 'advising' replaces 'counselling', and curative measures are meted out rather than preventive means taken.

Some pertinent questions are: Did Gane really benefit from the 'eastern counselling? Indeed, he topped the academic results—a commendable metamorphosis from a hotel boy to an academic top scorer. Or was he just a scoring machine? What befell his personality? Is Gane today, like life's many top scorers, a timid liver?

The timidity in living is the sour aftertaste of being subjected to brute force—corporal punishment, for example. India's Kamala Das writes about her husband's carnal force and its impact: 'Cowering / Beneath your monstrous ego, I ate the magic loaf and Became a dwarf.'

The feeling of being dwarfed is the undoing in growing up. The tender minds of the school-goers, when subjected to brute force—whatever the justification—feel dwarfed and timid. Such dwarfs are incapable of initiative and creativity.

As in the case of Kamala Das, the redeeming approach towards an erring scholar is empathy and dialogue, all non-judgemental. The Nobel Laureate Bertrand Russell says:

> If you have the sort of liking for children that many people have for horses or dogs, they will be apt to respond to your suggestions, and to accept prohibitions, perhaps with some good-humoured grumbling, but without resentment . . . Teachers who have this quality will seldom need to interfere with children's freedom, but will be able to do so, when necessary, without causing psychological damage . . . No rules, however wise, are a substitute for affection and tact.

Being tactful and affectionate presupposes the readiness to listen. Our availability for listening, and our listening comprehension skills themselves, are at sorry ebb. Naturally, 'counselling' degrades to 'advising', and our sons and daughters dread such word grilling. Grilling is not equal to (Western) counselling. If it is, Eastern counselling is preferable.

31

Keep Your Fork; the Best Is yet to Come

'Death, thou shalt die,' warned the crazy, metaphysical John Donne in his sonnet 'Death, Be Not Proud'. In the Oriental belief of the post-mortem *Nirvana*, death does not exist. In the Occidental, and Christian belief too, death is a stepping stone to eternal life. To the Buddhist's Right Understanding, we should welcome death not as an end but as rebirth, a beginning. It is the consolation of 'The best is yet to come'.

The elderly woman in Roger William Thomas's tale, 'Keep Your Fork' asks her pastor, who has gone to her for the last unction, to let her hold a fork in her right hand when people lay her dead body in the coffin.

To the curious pastor, she narrates a small experience of hers. In a party, after all the main courses of the menu were over and done, the host came to her, leant over, and said, 'Keep your fork; the best is yet to come.'

The 'best' could be a dessert, a pudding, or the like.

The pastor gets the resounding meaning of the little tale and feels humbled in his puny understanding of God's love after death.

Death is not a full stop. Death ushers in a new beginning, and so the fork symbolizes the best that is yet to come—the rebirth, the rejuvenation, and even *nirvana*. The dead person has completed her race and now is proceeding to win the laurels from the Almighty. Saint Augustine of Hippo puts it thus: 'And our heart is restless until it rests in you.' The restlessness is akin to that of the tumbling rivers until their waters get calm, when they merge in the ocean from which, in fact, they were birthed. So death should not be dreaded and distanced, but to be welcomed and espoused.

In that sense, dying is not terrible, but not dying is. Mortals unknowingly long for immortality. Lord Tennyson describes the burning pain of Tithonus (brother of King Priam of Troy) caused by immortality sans youthfulness. The dawn goddess, Eos, who has borne Tithonus a son, gets from gods immortality for her lover. But, in the absence of youthfulness, he withers into a despicable old man and later a grasshopper. To him, the grass-covered graves are happier homes than those of living men, because the dead enjoy rest for their bones and souls. Jealous of their lot, and terribly fed up with his immortality, he implores, 'Release me, and restore me to the ground.'

The classics tell us of the terrible times when Death is dead. Sisyphus, the king of Korinth, once tricked the god of Death, Thanatos. When Thanatos approached him with his chain to take away his life, Sisyphus asked him to try the chain on the god himself to test its power. Thanatos did it, and in the process Sisyphus bound him. Thenceforth, there were no more deaths. Ares, seeing none of his enemies in the battle die, rushed for Zeus's help and at last untied Thanatos. The chief god, Zeus, had a tough time maintaining the universe without a single person dying. Thus, death is an essential factor for the equilibrium of existence.

The Hindu gods had similar hard times, when Lord Yama (the god of death) was burned into ashes by Lord Shiva's anger-fire that emanated from his third eye. The barren Mrikanda, a devotee of Lord Shiva, got a boon—either a brilliant, smart son who would live a short life or a morose, weak son who would live long. Mrikanda opted for a good son of a short life span. Markandeya, the son, thus had only fifteen years of life on earth. Upon his parents' advice, he went on praying to and worshipping Lord Shiva. In the fifteenth year, when Lord Yama came with his noose of rope, the boy became so scared that he rushed and held fast on the Shivalinga. When Lord Yama cast his noose on the boy's neck, unfortunately it fell on the Shivalinga. Lord Shiva, in his immense fury, opened his third eye and burned Yama into ashes. Thenceforth, there were no deaths. Lord Indra and other gods became restless. Nobody was dying on earth. Absence of death posed a great threat to human existence itself. Upon other gods' request, Lord Shiva revived Death.

Deathlessness was the punishment given to Ashwathama by Lord Krishna, and the *Mahabharatha* says it was the severest punishment of all. As Ashwathama killed the Pandavas' sons and later the foetus of Parikshit, Arjun's grandson, Lord Krishna cursed him by saving him from death—he became a *chiranjeevi,* the ever-living. He had to roam about the world as an old man. This state, similar to Tithonus', was a traumatic experience.

Then, does not the sense in the Sanskrit mantra contradict what we have been discussing? *Mrutyorma amritam gamaya,* meaning, 'Lead me from mortality to immortality'. Here 'immortality' stands for 'nirvana', meaning one need not undergo the cycle of birth-rebirth.

The long and short of it all is that we should keep the fork; the best is yet to come. Shying away from thoughts of death is not the answer; on the contrary, it is repression. Having pleasant thoughts about death and thus being ready for it is the answer. As W. B. Yeats visualized, after this mortal dress(body) dissolves, the mire and fury disappears, and we will be reborn into a state of fire—rebirth into the angelic form.

About the Author

Born and brought up in a rich Christian ethos in Kerala, India, Jose K. C. has had a variety of life experiences, especially as a teacher. He is in the twenty-fifth year of his career as a teacher and educator. He is a popular orator, an inspiring teacher, and an original thinker.